ADDICTED TO DICK

2018 EDITION

"A very serious subject, life and death"

ELIZABETH WILEY MA JD, POMO ELDER

www.trafford.com
North America & international
toll-free: 1 888 232 4444 (USA & Canada)
fax: 812 355 4082

ADDICTED TO DICK 2018 Edition

Talking to a Social Service Director about the huge issues of children being abused, tortured, and often killed by boyfriends of their mothers, and often WITH their mother taking part in the torture and abuse, often for a man who is freeloading on HUD, or other public housing and welfare checks of the mother, we have decided to reissue ADDICTED TO DICK. To offer a new Court Mandated set of classes to remind women that being addicted to a man, no matter how awful he is, and how much he harms her, her children and even family members who are injured or murdered when they try to intervene that it is THEIR responsibility to keep their children, and themselves safe.

This book is written for use in Court Mandated programs, in lock downs for mothers jailed, their children taken away, and for self help before one more child is abused, or murdered. This book is written in a straight forward street level way for women to get it.

The original material is contained in this book, as the underlying addiction to a man, any man, is the cause of the horror these children suffer in their short lives. The Twelve Step program Parents Anonymous was started by a woman who witnessed her boyfriend murder one of her children, in front of her other children, and who then threatened to murder any of them who said a word to anyone about the situation. It is heavily suggested that women in Court mandated programs also join or form their own Parents Anonymous groups before one or more of your children is molested, abused or murdered by you and your boyfriend. MAKE NO MISTAKE ABOUT IT, if you let anyone, including yourself physically, mentally, emotionally, sexually harm your children YOU are guilty of a CRIME. This is not a childish game of not wanting others to "tell you what to do" or "who to love" A man who abuses you, and/or your children do NOT love you and is mentally ill.

There was a television movie made about a real life story of a young man who one day in the cafeteria at high school heard the other students joking about bloody worms at the spaghetti served that day for lunch. He threw plates on the floor, threw over tables, threw chairs at people and was arrested for violent and strange behavior. One social worker could NOT give up on the youngster, and finally, working with a therapist and the boy himself found out he had witnessed one of HIS mother's boyfriends murder his little sister by beating her head in with a heavy wrought iron frying pan. He had finally told the social worker that the "bloody worms" reminded him of her tiny brain smashed on the floor before he and his siblings were told they too would be killed if they ever said a word about what they witnessed. Before her tiny body was scrubbed off the kitchen floor and into a trash sack and the floor cleaned by his mother under threat of bodily harm to her and the others, all the children were made too afraid to ever say a word.

These truths are so horrible, but they have to be brought out to the women (and men) who let others, often abusive spouses, or parents who had once abused THEM, not just boyfriends. Talking about the numbers with the Social Services Director, we asked how many are there, I said maybe three million, he said, I think that may be too small a number.

America has to do better than this for our smallest citizens.

Mothers have to do better than this for their children. With the drug crisis in America we also have to realize what women will allow to be done, to their children and themselves, to keep drug pushers or men who will provide them with drugs coming back with drugs.

NOTE: Many men allow women to torture, abuse, neglect and kill their children as well, but this book is FOR a court mandatory women's program.

Police, teachers, hospital staff, family members NEED to have the support to get help for the families in which these things happen, we do NOT need forty MORE years of hearings and nicely catered panel meetings, we NEED to protect our children.

SPECIAL NOTE: Many of the women arrested for these crimes have been abused, molested and beaten and tortured or seen their Mothers and siblings abused, tortured, molested or murdered as children. It is time as a nation to point those remaining fingers at OURSELVES and put a stop to this horror. NOT punish, or stupid cop show "get the bad guys", STOP these situations from happening. We NEED faster, better family support programs, and we NEED better mental health for violent people and ANYONE who allows a child, or themselves to be abused in any way.

As sad as it sounds, many of the men and women who torture, molest and murder babies and children were abused themselves as children. Many of them in the foster care systems.

WE, as parents, as a NATION have to take the blinders off and resolve these issues, and inspire other countries to resolve them forever from the face of the earth.

Dedication:

Dedicated to the women who have been Court Mandated and put up with my rudeness and intervention into their lives on behalf of their own safety and the safety of their children.

So many of them have worked hard, in this, and other Domestic Violence programs that are Court Mandated.

Very special dedication to my two sons: Tim and Dean, my amazing miracles. Without you I never would have made it. The laughter, the love, the wisdom, the disagreements. I love you both.

Thank you for the care and help of my Credit Union Director Cindy and Dani for all the support and help to take loans and believe in myself to write books to help others have better lives.

Thank you to my neighbor Mark Lamonica, photographer and author of Junk Yard Dogs, and Rio L.A. an L A Times Book of the Year, a special thank you for never allowing me to give up on writing my programs into books and using them for my work.

Thank you to all my family and friends for the cards, and gifts I bought, and forgot in drawers, or my truck or at the stable when a crisis came up. Thank you all for reminding me that there are some happy wonderful people who deal, no matter what the pain in life.

Other special dedications:

This is the page where it gets difficult, there are so many to thank, my publishing helpers, and designers,

The women who gave me life, wisdom, strength, who learned from their mistakes, and helped me to learn from and not be defeated by mine.

My Grandmothers, My Mom, My Step-Mothers, My Aunts, my sisters, cousins, and adopted daughter, Sam, my nieces and daughter in laws, and all of our family. The love, laughter, disagreements, how would my life be without you coming as you did when the boys were grown and out making their own ways, no time for Mom. Thank Larry and Rudy for trusting you to me when it was necessary.

To Margot How could I have ever made it through being devastatingly disabled without your leadership and inspiration along with the others in the adult acquired brain injury groups. How could I have made it through the cancer of my beautiful sixteen year old son, and years of relapse and treatment if I had not seen you go through it with grace and love for your daughter when she had brain tumors. How could I have made it through the despair of my younger son as he felt so helpless with his Mom and brother disabled and nothing he could do. Your strength and guidance always reminding me that our strength comes from God, not ourselves.

To Auntie Lizzie who taught me a man is just what he is, and not to expect more than any man can give, to know that the most perfect man can die, become injured, or get PTSD and leave you to support not just yourself and the children, but him as well. To be prepared, and not to fill my own life with bitterness and anger, live just is.

To my students, riding students and horsey-friends. I know you all gave me more than I gave you.

And of course thanks to my wonderful animals, you never cared if I lost my job, my health, my career, my youthful appearance, as long as I had hay, pet food, and lots of pets and love. And of course for all the love and healing you have given the students, veterans and first responders in our programs over the years.

Thank you all.

AN EXPLORATION OF WOMEN'S ADDICTION TO MEN

A VERY SPECIAL NOTE:

VETERANS: Whether you are a veteran, a spouse or child of a veteran, or a parent, neighbor, or friend of a veteran, IF YOU SEE physical abuse, PLEASE take time to talk to the person or ask the police for help.

PLEASE if you are a veteran, and your spouse or children, siblings, or parents are complaining and saying you have assaulted them, go to the VA and do not take NO for an answer. GET HELP.

There are veteran support programs at many community centers, colleges, and most VFW Posts and American Legion Posts have senior members who have dealt with this problem for members for decades. I prefer VFW and American Legion, many of their members have dealt with so many others they have great immediate connections to get help foryou.

IT IS SERIOUS. Often veterans suffering from untreated PTSD are unaware of some things they are doing, and NEED professional combat veterans to help them find the right help.

Active duty as well.

PLEASE be aware that sometimes spouses, partners, and children will NEVER trust you again, that is NOT their responsibility, nor your fault, but what has happened is real, do not let it go any farther. This is not about whether people love you, or even if they wonder if you love them, it is about a serious and possibly deadly form of PTSD.

If YOU find yourself places and have no idea how you got there, or where hours, or days have passed, or if others ask you about things you do not remember, GET HELP. This too is a serious and dangerous form of PTSD.

IF you feel you "might" lose control, go somewhere and contact a VA crisis line, and/or find a VFW support person to help you get help before something bad happens.

FIRST RESPONDERS: CRITICAL CARE DOCTORS, NURSES PLEASE take note: these forms of PTSD are not limited to combat soldiers. First Responders have told us that they have been promised for years that departments would add programs to help them without forcing them out of the careers they love and that motivate them.

SOMETHING has to be done, but it is not worth harming or killing members of your family, or innocent people doing things you may not even remember.

WE AMERICANS need to take a world lead in helping our active duty, veterans, and first responders find a resolution to the deep heartbreaking and mind numbing injuries they suffer, now named PTSD. New neurological research is being done that proves some of what has been diagnosed as PTSD is in fact a type of neurological order related to head injuries and percussion injuries to the brain from gun shots, and other loud percussion realities in both war, and critical citizen care first response jobs.

Often, meditation, group talks, sweat lodges and other alternate programs help active duty, first responders, and veterans to heal BEFORE they harm themselves or others.

Sadly, both men and women veterans are among those arrested for harming children and spouses, siblings or parents when untreated for PTSD. PLEASE take time to get help.

Many veteran groups and active duty groups are demanding a more positive help for stress for their membership. Asking for help should NEVER permanently shut a veteran, first responder, or active duty person from their career. The First Responders often ARE veterans, or active Reserve troops and should all be able to have fast, supportive help when they are pushed to their limits. NOT made afraid to ask for help, because they will lose their careers, and be labeled as mentally ill, and put on medications that as they say, turn them into "zombies" and effectively make them sad disabled people with no hope.

TAKE THE ADDICTED TO DICK QUIZ

Are you in a relationship where the most active part of the real relating is in your imagination

Are you in a relationship where the most active part of the relating is the police the neighbors keep calling for "disturbances" at your house and one or both of you get arrested

Are you in a relationship where your medical bills are mounting up due to abuse

Are you in a relationship where there are one or more affairs on each side of the bed

Are you in a relationship that is number 227 or more since high school, and you are only 21

Do you think about romance more than your job, your family, school, your friends, or even the man you are now dating or married to

Do you believe there is just ONE perfect man out there who will make your life complete and in that 227 + you have just not found him

Do you believe that when you do find that knight in shining armor your life will be perfect

Do you have major crushes on rock stars, movie stars, or other celebrities even while in a relationship, or married, and you are over 13

Do you think there is no real reason for YOU to do well in high school, or college or career because the perfect man is out there who will take care of you

Do you think if you just find the right hairstyle, make-up, underwear, or can just slip your size twelve (normal body size) into a size two (non-existent, except for a thirteen year old undernourished BOY, or a small number of women who are less than four feet tall and come from countries where starvation has been ongoing for centuries so have tiny, frail bones...the right man will be there and want to take care of you

If you have answered ANY of these question yes, you need to assess your wise thoughts on relationships. This book has a funny title, there is nothing funny about it. You are suffering, the man is probably suffering, and anyone who has to relate to you is suffering, your children may be more than suffering, they may be being molested, tortured, and in danger of being killed. As addictive as heroin, or gambling, or any other addictive and destructive behavior, IF addiction to men has taken over your life, you need to have knowledge and support to face the facts, and to heal yourself.

CAUTION: DO NOT TAKE VIOLENCE OR THREATS OF VIOLENCE LIGHTLY either to yourself, your family, or especially your children.

Domestic Violence Programs do NOT recommend couples counseling unless and until both parties have completed and healed with individual therapy to identify and resolve their own issues, such as what gave them the idea it was OK to either be abused, or to abuse anyone. Anger management and conflict resolution classes can help both parties to learn to communicate without violence, or other forms of abuse. PLEASE shop wisely for programs, there are many that are nothing more than man hater clubs, and they are NOT going to help you identify your own issues and resolve your addiction to abusive men.

Violence is a choice. VERY few domestic violence Court mandated programs clients act the way they do with the person they abuse, verbally, physically, financially, emotionally as they do with business, social, or family acquaintances.

Make no mistake about it, there are violent women in straight and gay relationships as well, but this book is a Court mandated program for women who have lost their children due to their allowing boyfriends (or female partners) to abuse and or kill their children.

Often abusers are thought of as the nicest of people by family, friends and neighbors. Even close family members are unaware of the hidden demons in an abuser. Sadly, over the decades of facilitating Domestic Violence Court Mandated programs I have met both men and women who are apparently completely unaware that they are violent. While some are manipulators, and apologize and say "they lost it", there are some people who appear quite normal on their jobs, and even they do not know what happened. It is up to the victims to recognize this and stay away from that person. There are others that require safe housing due to their level of violence when someone they think they "own" has left them. This is an increasing problem for women veterans and first responders with PTSD.

A victim HAS to acknowledge the reality of the danger and keep the children safe, and herself safe. Get professional help, too many families are in the news being murdered by violent and out of control partners or husbands who will kill anyone in the way of their getting their family back.

Even if a person is pushed to self defense, a MAN, or a professionally trained woman, such as military, veteran, or first responder, has NO RIGHT to hit a woman or child. If a person has made another person mad enough to even want to cause violence, the person needs to LEAVE the situation and get help.

Women victims, or mothers, can NOT excuse the violent behavior, and has to realize that it is in her own best interest, and that of her children to get away from a violent person, or let them go. Too many women are assaulted, or worse, hit by cars chasing an angry man down the street when he walks out to cool off. LET HIM GO.

VIOLENCE IS A CHOICE: There may be a small number of men or women who have brain injuries, or neurological damage that are unable to control themselves. It may seem sad, and mean to get out of that relationship, but your duty is to your children and to yourself. We work with veterans and it is hard to get many of them to understand they can NOT put children and women at risk because of their physical disability.

Many programs are beginning to help families of veterans and others with brain injuries to deal with these issues in the most positive ways possible. These are NOT easy choices or realities. Children and women deserve to be protected from violence even if the person is NOT responsible for the cause of that violence.

This brings alcohol and drugs as excuses. I have my own opinion. The FIRST time a person is violent, or a bully while drinking or using drugs, NO excuse, but maybe a waiver if they NEVER drink or take drugs again. IF that person drinks or takes drugs again, it is time to say GOOD BYE to protect yourself and your children.

IF a person knows they can cause harm to another if they drink or take drugs, it is a CHOICE to not ever take them again OR to get into a treatment program that helps them to never use them again. YOU do not have the right to inflict this person on your children, and if you NEED an abusive drunk or drug addict so much it is OK for him to harm you, this book is for you, get help, get free, and learn to be loved, not just needy enough to be abused.

THIS MEANS PRESCRIPTIONS AS WELL.

I do not believe God put any person on this earth to be abused, in any way, by any other person.

Being abused is a choice as well. Domestic Violence programs differ in their concepts of this, and most agree that research has shown most women need straight forward self centered mental health treatment to help them NEVER accept any form of abuse or allow any form of abuse to their children.

SPARE THE ROD and SPOIL THE CHILD. This is a horror and a misstatement of the Bible. The rod discussed was NOT a stick or bat to beat your wife or children with, it was, in context with the times, the curved rod a SHEPHERD used to guide sheep and goats, and to help recover them when they are stuck on a steep mountain size or fallen into a ditch. The shepherds did NOT beat their sheep or goats. The statement later, related to a child means to take the time it takes to watch and guide a child, and to use the "rod" to bring that child back on the path. Do NOT allow yourself or anyone else to excuse beating your child or you with the Bible.

WOMEN SHOULD DO WHAT THE MAN SAYS. Proverbs in particular is very clear that a man should guide and care for his family, but it is clear and says to treat ones spouse with love and care, and gratitude for what she gives to you as a life help mate, NOT a slave, or abused mother of the kids to keep them out of the man's way.

While a woman may not know HOW to leave, or may not be able to deal with the stress and fear of no man, it is important to admit that and deal with the real issues, not just stay until the next beating of yourself or your children occurs.

A friend's sister called and told her she had left her husband. He hit her ONCE. She packed up the kids, moved to another city, asked for a transfer in her job. He did get help, and it turned out he had a brain tumor. While she let the children see him when he was able, it was never overnight, or alone. At first he was very angry, and hurt. Later he realized she did what was really best for the family. He died. What would have been the point of staying with a dying man, no matter how sad, if he was harming her, or the children. SHE knew that one hit was more than enough and that was that.

Many women need to ask themselves to get the help they need to stand up for themselves and their children. It may take time in therapy to find out why, and to find a new self that will learn to identify situations and NOT be with a man who might be violent. How many women come into Court Mandated programs, the third, fifth, tenth wife or girlfriend of a man who beat his other wives, girlfriends and children. Learn to ask WHY this perfect man, if he IS so perfect, has not been snapped up by other women, or why his other wives and girlfriends are ALL long gone.

One of my Aunts, after her daughter told her she just did not "understand" the man she "loved" said to her, and I have never forgotten it some wise words. She said do NOT come back a year or more from now when your fun loving, bar hopping great guy, is out bar hopping, being fun loving, while YOU are at home with sick kids, no food, and the car he wrecked drunk driving. Her daughter was angry, but did eventually stop seeing that perfect man. She later married a really nice guy who had a job, money for a home when they married, and they are still married, almost forty years later, nice grandparents.

It is your choice. Take the time to heal yourself, and to find out what good relationships are, NOT romance from movies, celebrity stories, music videos and grocery store romance books.

DO NOT EXPECT MEN TO BE ROMANTIC

One of the first things most domestic violence programs teach is the more the gifts, the more the romantic dinners, the more is being hidden.

Much better to go have a burger with a grease covered guy who is working on his car, boat or motorcycle than to eat a romantic candle light dinner that cost as much as the car repairs, and get beaten up later that night.

NOT to say turn it down if your husband, or boyfriend takes you out now and then, but those slick guys who are "romantic" usually are too good to be true.

My family and friends have many couples who have had marriages of fifty years or more, and STILL loved each other. Others 25 to 30 years where cancer, or accidents ended the marriage, but at the end, they STILL loved each other.

Most men think if they don't burp after their beer after work they are romantic, and if they let you sit near the living room if you are quiet while they watch football it shows how much they care. GO OUT WITH YOUR SISTERS and FRIENDS. Once we had a friend who was whining about her husband not being romantic. I asked, what is good about him? She listed a lot of things.

We decided to cheer her up. We gave her what we decided to call a "romance" basket. We got champagne flutes, nice placemats, candle holders and candles and a little vase she could put flowers in at every meal. We said, he probably will not even notice, and you will have all you want. He actually liked it, and we also gave her some candles for the bathroom, some bubble bath, and said go take care of you instead of stewing. He actually came and washed her back from time to time. Everyone liked it so much, we used to put together the baskets and sell them for fundraisers for our women's groups at church and community groups.

One of my friends was super rich, her husband told her she could buy anything she wanted, she had credit cards, cash, bank accounts, and accounts at all the best stores. He gave her a new sports car every single year, even after he passed away his business manger traded her car in for anything she wanted. SHE wanted a dozen red roses. YEARS she wanted those roses. He said, call the florist, buy ten dozen. One birthday I bought her a dozen red roses, from that florist, in their special gold box. He came home and saw those flowers. He said who bought those, she said Liz. He said WHY. She said because she heard me keep on whining about them all these years so bought them. From that day on, he at least had the secretary send her roses of different seasonal colors in gold boxes. OR, once in awhile, he even stopped and bought them himself! Now that was romantic.

To think your husband is going to come off the freeway, or off ten hours of construction work, or fixing cars, or working in an office and wash, put on a tux and dance around the living room with a rose in his teeth is not realistic.

To see a man walking with his wife, her hair all gone, her little radiation cap on her head, shrunken by chemo to a stick with skin, and see clearly that he LOVES her, that is romantic. When your head is in the toilet throwing up with the flu, and he takes the kids out fishing, or to dinner at his Mom's, or YOUR Moms, that is romantic.

Some men are better in the romantic department, some not so much. Be grateful for the love of a man who goes to work every day and brings home the money, and you KNOW in those favorite old college athletic shorts, and ripped football jersey that he is NOT out finding someone to have a quickie with behind the dumpster at the car parts store.

NOW you can STOP looking at, or for romantic heels. OF COURSE they can afford expensive restaurants, and new suits, and expensive cologne, THEY are not supporting you and do not intend to. Whether it is $400 a week salary, or a few million a year, a man who uses his money to care for you and the kids.......THAT is romantic. Save your own money and take your sister or your Mom on a cruise, even with the kids they are fun, and who knows, no romance man might miss you enough to pick a flower out of your yard and clean up the house before you get home. Man clean, not woman clean. My daughter in laws thanked me because I had taught my sons that the toilet and shower need to be cleaned out a couple of times a week. Most men think if they picked up the towels and left them for you to wash they have real reason to be proud of their love and care for you.

Men are NOT psychics. DO NOT expect your man should know what you want. In groups over the decades women have complained that their man did not give them what they wanted. Like the red roses. In many cases the group would ask, did you ever TELL HIM. Most of the time, nope. HE SHUD know. SHUD is a four letter word in relationships. One woman always got beautiful expensive jewelry, BUT she said, she liked silver, he kept giving her gold. Did she ever tell him. NOPE. She thought he would have his feelings hurt. What we asked did she think it did when she had a jewelry box full of lovely gifts she NEVER wore.

One of my sisters had a husband who was ex military and he liked the clothes folded a certain way, she said, fine, I will clean the bathrooms, YOU fold the clothes. It worked for over 25 years before she passed away from leukemia. WORK out the problems. There are great classes and books on family negotiations. Teach the methods to your children, their teen years will be so much more peaceful.

I read once that you know you are a couple when your husband buys things for the house or car for your holiday presents. I guess I was beloved. I got a wonderful carburetor one Christmas, and when I got home from work, most of the engine was on a tarp in the living room so he could watch the fishing shows. I did ask if it might be easier if we got a cable box in the garage. He laughed. My carburetor, on his truck, worked so well when we went fishing. Romance.

I think romance can be a value we CHOOSE to define ourselves. Not little old maids, or even teams of both men and women who write grocery store cheap romance books. Curled up next to a clean, just showered man, watching a movie I call THE movie (you know the same old car chases, shoot 'em up, blow 'em up, women running around in short skirts and heels and of course SCREAMING). Reading a book, or doing nothing is more romantic to me than wondering where a man who cheats all the time is, and why you are not "good enough for him". It is more romantic than sitting across the table from an irritable man in a tux, or nice suit who keeps huffing and puffing and looking at his watch. There are men who love to dine out, as opposed to shoving down three man sized meals while driving home from the drive thru. Take the time to find them, if you can NOT live without those dinners, you will be happier, and so will any man you have chosen to leave alone rather than attempt to change into the guy on the cover of that grocery store romance.

BEWARE: Any man who seems too good to be true, probably is. When you are fourteen and want to tell all your friends you have an "adult" boyfriend who has a great car, STOP. Ask yourself if this guy is such a catch, how come he is not snapped up by a woman is own age. The answer is because a woman his age sees he lives at home in his parent's garage or grandmother's basement A woman his age sees he still thinks he is the high school jock, and keeps getting fired from dead end, going nowhere jobs that will NEVER lead him to be a stable and responsible partner or PARENT for a child.

A woman his age is smart enough to KNOW that "bareback" is NOT the best way to get pregnant and dumped. Unlike you.

This same man is the good dancing, cool drink buying guy you pick up at the bar. ALL the other women there say NO THANKS. The MEN there look at you and say NO THANKS. They get it, you are a quick trip to prison and a lifetime of being a registered sex offender.

The law did NOT make the law so YOU can not have sex with the greatest guy God ever invented. The law is there to protect dummies from getting into messes with child molesters.

AND models are people who have AGENTS, actresses are people who AGENTS. When you get an audition it is at a HUGE cattlecall that your AGENT takes you to, or has security and hundreds of models or actresses going on and off the stage with a quick "thank you for your time" if you have any kind of attitude that see will cost them money because they need professionals who do the job, not skanks who can NOT do the job and cost them retake after retake.

NO ONE, not the most celebrated of celebrities or riches of producers, is going to give you a role and career for a blow job. YES, there are people out there who managed to get a few roles, even big ones, but sooner or later, someone discovers, they are skanks and do NOT get the job done and are costing the companies money. A retake often costs hundreds of thousands of dollars.

SO, save your life, and do not get trapped into being sex trafficked in pornography, or giving a blow job or being raped in a hotel by a guy who promises you a career or role. TELL YOUR AGENT, is what our agents told us, those type of men get blacklisted from any contact with REAL models and actresses.

The world is filled with pathetic used up, usually drunken or drugged up skanks, a lot more of them show up buried in shallow graves by "photographers" who convince them they are dong a shoot in the mountains, or desert and rape and kill them instead.

BE SMART.

AUTHOR'S NOTE

This is a book that discusses the use of twelve steps to address addiction to men. It is NOT based on any current Twelve Step program that exists: It is NOT a Twelve Step program book. Each of the steps of those programs have been examined for use with addictions of many kinds and is a suggested thought to help women deal with their addiction to men who put them, and their children at risk. The suggestion is to find a Twelve Step program for women addicted to alcohol, or drugs, or gambling, shopping, or any other thing and just add your addiction to men in while going through the program, Most women find, as my Dad said when he was running Twelve Step programs and decided to separate the men and women, the women are as addicted to dick as they are to substance abuse and they were getting used by the men in the programs. Get involved, find a therapist and grow yourself well.

If you have children, and can find a Parents Anonymous, please join and get help before one of your children is tortured or killed by the man you are currently addicted to.

You can do the work in this book alone, or find any Twelve Step program and move through the steps with a sponsor. It is more tan likely if you are addicted to dick, you will find other areas where you are either fully addicted, or on the borderline. Twelve Steps work because of the interaction with others who have addictions and the need to change their lives and are ready to do it.

Any addiction work or program is best worked together. Find some other women who are also addicted, Work together. The original Founding members of AA, the first Twelve Step program got together and created a way to help themselves, each other, and eventually added the Twelfth Step, the Step that leads one to take the relief and serenity of regaining control of your life to others who are still suffering.

Weight Watchers was originally founded by a group of women who had tried every diet, exercise plan, gone to diet farms, and fat camps, and starved and binged, and could NOT reach a normal weight. They worked with their doctors, and each other to not give up and figure out how to lose weight. This is an inspiration for working together and finding a way with others in the same boat as you find yourself.

The Seven Day Plan in the second portion of this book is based on a stop smoking program invented by a doctor. It was revised by others for use in ridding themselves of other addictive disorders and behaviors, or just to change life for the better.

These are just suggestions for those afflicted to find HOPE.

This author has been involved in Twelve Step programs for decades, initially for eating disorders brought on in the modeling industry. They did NOT have undereaters Anonymous, so I joined Overeaters Anonymous. It made no sense, but eventually did, that whether over eating, or not eating due to stress or pressure from my career agent and corporations I worked for, I found the underlying problem was inside each of us, and could be healed by Higher Power. Then we decided to utilize a quasi twelve step program for youth and foster children or probation lock down clients. Finding peace in the programs, the youth told us they needed it earlier, so KIDS ANONYMOUS created KIDS JR. We asked the Anonymous Headquarters in New York how we became a real twelve step, they said, send a copy of your program by email, and that is that. Kids helping other kids has shown us such great success, it gives us great inspiration to suggest the use of twelve step materials and groups for many of life's realities to find the courage to face our problems, the serenity to deal, with those we can correct, and those we have to learn to let go, and the wisdom to know the difference.

As noted in the introduction, Addicted to Dick 2018 Edition came about because our Court Mandated Program directors were complaining that their programs were not working and more and more children were being placed in foster care, parental rights terminated and the children adopted out, or the children were molested, tortured, abused and even murdered by the boyfriends (and spouses) of women who did not seem to have the courage or insight to protect their children.

WE dedicate this new edition to Gabriel, and to Jonathan, murdered in our local country in 2018, and to the other estimated 3 million children who will be grievously injured, or killed by their Mother's boyfriend, and even their Mother so she does not lose "her man" by telling him to get out.

ADDICTED TO DICK

The reason this book exists is having seen the bad relationships, the effect on the children, and the continued diving into worse situations by women and girls while volunteering as a Court Mandated Domestic Violence Facilitator for both public and expensive, prestigious private programs, I realized this is NOT about money, race, education, or whether you Mom was abused or not. There was something unique for each woman. It takes time to figure it out.

One Three Tiered project was built to address the issues, but the developer ripped off the charity and city program, somehow managing to force the sale of the land and program buildings into a NO BID sale and buying buildings and land worth millions of dollars for pennies on the dollars to create his own private financial growth package.

We began to notice that many of the women were as addicted to men as they were to substance abuse, or addictions to food, gambling, shopping, hoarding, over cleaning, or living in squalor, addicted to raising hell at the school, using your child to go cause trouble with adults to feed a never ending fight with authority figures, exercise, being the neighborhood or family gossip or bully, we said lets ask the women and girls to help us create success for themselves.

Washing the dishes too much (ask your family, and friends, are you the one who grabs away their plate while they are still eating), cleaning the house too much, scrubbing spots on the family laundry too much can all be addictions. Yelling at your children or husband or the pets can be addictions as well. Dry alcoholism, as described in Al-Anon is another form of addiction that leads to unsafe, or unhappy behaviors. Most of us know at least one woman who is more annoying, or heartbreaking, or both with her constant tale of abusive relationships, these behaviors can be more unhealthy and upsetting than using drugs or alcohol to friends and family. WORK does NOT appreciate abusive, violent, and at times deadly relationships charging into work to harm innocent members of the staff. Recently a whole school was locked down, children shot and teachers shot, some persons killed by the estranged husband of one of the teachers. This book is about looking to see if we might be one of those women, and looking for help to stop putting ourselves, our children and others at risk.

This is NOT blaming the abused woman or girl. It is asking the abused woman or girl to realize how and why these things come into her life and help her get them out.

Reading some of the books and materials by Al-Anon, or Parents Anonymous helps one realize that just because YOU are not the drunk, or drug addict, or violence addict does not mean you are not addicted, or a dry alcholic.

Rehabilitation programs, both in hospital and out patient support, as well as programs of the Anonymous Twelve Step programs have been created for those addicted. For those who use substances, or activities, or even inactivity to soothe, or control not just their own lives, but often the lives of other get a new attitude towards people who use violence as a way to soothe themselves and control their own lives and those of others. One must learn about oneself, and recognize addictions, admit addictions and get into a daily working program to assist in recovering from those addictions. The goal is to finally take real control over one's life, and maybe find balance and self love enough to build a calm, and rewarding life, and maybe find a TRUE partnership and life long relationship, not a romance, or vision that is not attainable any more than spending the rent money on gambling, or the lottery in the dim chance that you might "win". Without the wisdom and change in life behaviors, just as many lottery winners, a good period might come by, but in a couple of years, back to the same old losing and self harming way of life.

How do YOU view yourself, men, marriage and family life

In domestic violence projects, the first support project is often to draw a picture of yourself, stick figures are perfect. One woman described herself as "little". Another screamed out that her parents needed to stop treating such a "little" person so badly. She was in fact quite large, long gone from her parents home, and the mother of four. Another drew herself as a tiny child, finger in corner of her mouth, leg twisted to the side as a shy child. This woman was in fact a powerful executive, one of few women in her field, and had no qualms about calling high powered executives and politicians and making demands as needed for her work.

Draw yourself here. THEN take a selfie on your phone.........
how do they compare.

Draw, paste pictures, create a collage of what you really want to be in life.

Draw, paste pictures, create an image of what you can do to reach your goals.

BE honest with yourself about how you view yourself. It will help you start to realize why your life is chaotic and has a repetitive abuse theme or short lived relationships that you can realize you inflict on yourself. For example: There you are, on computer, online fantasies, rather than figuring out what you like to do, and going out and doing those things and find a partner who likes those things enough to be out doing them, instead of plotting how to get you to send money, or go meet him somewhere for quick sex while his wife or girlfriend is at work or out of town with her sick mother.

Draw yourself in relationships in the space below. How do you see yourself in position to your current spouse, or partner, your children, friends, parents, in laws, friends and boss and other employees. Use pictures, or write about these areas to find out how you see yourself. Pictures and selfies might also help you to see similarities as well as differences in what is real and what you see. There was an article in a weight loss class long ago about a very famous actress who before starting the program had wondered why people always thought she was fat. She got photographs, give for free for being in a prestigious beauty pageant qualifying cattle call. She slapped the pictures on the table and demanded her mother find out why they had sent her pictures of a fat woman. Her mother took her to a therapist, even confronted with the photographs and a mirror this size 22 XXX Large woman thought inside her mind she had been one of the best looking in the bikini line up and could not believe the fat woman in a laughable bikini was herself. She got a therapist, into a weight loss program, and went on to finish college and become a star. It was not easy, but she inspired many others.

You might then begin to write about who and what YOU really are. Look over the last pages, and see if you have changed your mind about who your saw yourself as being just a few pages ago.

Look in the mirror, take selfies. ASK others, and listen to what they tell you. It is hard, and it is more than likely going to be painful. You are urged to find a counselor to help you through this daring and courageous act of finding out who you really are, and who you really can be.

The next step is to write as fast as you can: Number one through ten, then fill in the blank:

A MAN IS:....................

Then:

A WOMAN IS:

Take time to look over your answers. If you did not answer as fast as possible, write one through ten again, and start over, use one word answers, use text message shortcuts, just be honest and get the immediate CORE thought out and on paper. Try it on a tape recorder or the recorder on your computer or phone. The important part is to say the first part over as fast as possible and add your own words or thoughts as needed AFTERWARD.

In domestic violence support groups I facilitated, and in discussions with several group leaders, we found the most common two phases for a man were:

A MAN IS AN ASSHOLE A MAN IS A PROVIDER

The two were often interchanged

In group we would then point out that it might be possible to see how men felt honored in any relationship with a woman whose whole attitude was GIVE ME THE CHECK YOU ASSHOLE. Often these are the same women and girls who profess to be waiting for the knight on a shining white horse going to take perfect care of them forever.

These same women often had very derogatory statements to say about women in their ten statements about women and girls. If a woman hates women, or hates being a woman or disrespects women, how is she going to become a self respecting woman, able to stand up for herself or her children when necessary. How can she find her own best self since she is a woman and thinks women are a lesser species?

CORE beliefs are those self statements we live by. Most people get to a mind set that they would rather be unhappy, abused, or have their children abused or murdered than to admit their core belief system might be wrong. Most people are unaware of their core beliefs, or even if they speak them outloud, unaware that is what they are trying hard to make true.

An interesting side note is that abusive men often use exactly the same derogatory terms to describe women as the women list themselves. However they may see themselves, often assholes is first on the list, they see women as manipulative, trapping, dishonest, cheating beings out to use up their hard earned money (even if it is from a trust fund and NOT earned) and spend a lot of it on useless horrible brats. No matter that those are his own children, worse if they are not.

Women often explained their term "asshole" as a jerk, who is abusive, stingy (even if he is giving all her has, no matter an unemployment or disability check or a massive executive salary), ugly, not romantic, and demands sex that does not satisfy her. Though the definitions are different, it would appear that any of these pairs would have a hard time creating a good marriage and family.

This would also seem to indicate that these couples are choosing each other to be right. This statement is described in domestic violence facilitator manuals as the need of both parties to be right rather than happy. Often in domestic violence relationships both partners are users, addicted, manipulators, and so involved in their own mess they can not care about each other or any children in the relationship.

One research point in the manuals, trained and used to help the women recognize their own need to change to avoid another abusive relationship if they manage to get out of the one they are Court Mandated into the programs to resolve. The manuals list research that has shown women, if given a football stadium filled to capacity with men who were all single, employed, stable and tens, except ONE, would find that one. Without sufficient counseling and participation in domestic violence programs and individualized therapy, this same woman has been shown over and over to find an even worse man the next time, the next, and the next. She will join the "man hater's club". She will die, suffer broken bones, commit crimes, go to prison, lose her family and friends, allow her children to be molested, abused, starved and even killed to NOT avail herself of a get of jail free card and get out of this self prophesizing membership in an awful club.

If you are addicted to dick, you need to find a domestic violence program, therapist, or women's support group and learn to understand yourself, and your choices. Taking responsibility is the first part of changing your life.

I do not believe anyone truly WANTS to be unhappy, or abused, or killed by someone they claim to love, and presumably who once loved them enough to get involved in a relationship. However, I do believe after years of training and seeing hundreds of women in these groups go by that whatever motivates each woman is more addicting than heroin.

Once while working in an emergency room I saw a woman admitted who had been stabbed in the stomach by her abusive boyfriend. The police officer who had accompanied her to the hospital said she did not have to worry, the man had been arrested and would serve long years for felony assault. I have never gotten over my shock when the woman cursed out the police officer, struggled off the gurney, and left the hospital against medical advice to go bail "her lover" out of jail. She returned to the hospital a few days later with a severe infection from the untreated stab wounds, apparently bailing out the boyfriend did not make him feel he owed her any duty to get her care. The last straw was she filed a law suit against the hospital for the infection, claiming they should have kept her there against her wishes. She lost.

DR. Phil McGraw has a series of books about self help, and I recommend them. If not them, find others, find a group, a therapist, or counselors and get help.

CAUTION: there are a lot of man haters out there passing themselves off as family counselors, women's counselors, and domestic violence professionals. It is a harsh reality that in a time of need you still have to be a wise shopper for the assistance you need.

Now that you have had time to look at your responses to A MAN IS…..and a WOMAN IS…. Try the same exercise with the statements on the next pages.

MARRIAGE IS:

A FAMILY IS……..

CHILDREN ARE.......

I HAD CHILDREN BECAUSE……..

Take a careful look at your answers. Again ask yourself if you were honest, or afraid someone might see what you wrote.

Are YOU afraid YOU might see what you wrote and what YOU really think?

Women have answered these question in the most negative of terms. If a woman thinks men are jerks who should support them, and rescue them from whatever reality means, but at the same time write that they think women are manipulators (yes, a lot of women think women are manipulators as their first choice of defining a woman)and worthless, and marriage is hell, a trap, a nightmare, and children are brats, lazy, ungrateful, selfish, and other negative responses and the only reason they had children was because their Mother wanted Grandchildren, they "got" pregnant as if it somehow came upon them in some unknown manner, or to get a man to marry them, how can a good marriage be expected to result. How can she even know what a good relationship is, or how to carry her part of a life partnership and family member?

On the other hand, I believe every woman has times when she hates being married, hates men and hates her children. I think that if honest, a woman keeps these moments to a minimum and learns or has already learned to experience the anger, boredom, disappointment and move past it. Knowing how to handle the feelings of frustration, loneliness, loss of self –centered gratification ALL of the time and no coping skills to balance the needs of self and those of others are all things that can be learned in domestic violence support programs, counseling and good marriage and family education programs.

CAUTION: if there is violence, it is time to get out. Give it a rest. BOTH of you need to work out your own issues before going to a professional to help you with reunification of your family, or how to create a happy extended family experience for you and your children. Divorce means dealing with EACH other, NOT trying to force your children to take sides, or be a harmed part of this experience. A Priest once wrote a book titled "Pictures from the Heart" and contained pictures of children to be shared with parents who were having issues, or divorcing. One of the pictures showed a child, with barbed wire wrapped around her heart, with her parents pulling the ends and shredding her heart.

If one or both parents are too addicted, or mentally ill, own it, and work with professionals to find a safe place for the children.

REALITY CHECK: You cannot FORCE anyone to love you. You might be able to manipulate them with money, sex, love (or what you pass off as love), since I believe love is not present in any form of abuse, whether verbal, physical, mental, financial, emotional or any other kind of way people manage to think up to "love" each other.

The sad reality is that many women who are addicted to dick may look back and over the ravages of relationships gone bad find many men who actually were unfortunate enough to really love them. To have had someone who loved you until you treated them so badly you finally drove them off is not anything to feel proud, or victimized about.

Men fall into these same realities, but this is a book about women addicted to dick, not men and their problems with women or women addiction. (THis is to fend off the tons of letters from women who want me to know that MEN are just as bad, or worse). That may be true, but regardless of what men do women who are addicted to dick is the subject of this book and not the men who have abused them.

SOME TOOLS THAT MIGHT HELP:

These are a run through of the author's idea of how to utilize a Step program as a way out of addiction to men. This is NOT an official Twelve Step program. There is NO Twelve Steps for men addiction. There are more than likely as many men who are addicted to women, and there is NO official Twelve Step program for men with woman addiction. There is NOT a man, or woman, in the world who can make YOUR life changes except YOU. There is NO ONE except YOU that can make your dreams come true, or your life a success and happy.

STEP ONE

Admit that my life is out of control. Admit that I am powerless over men, I have used my addiction to men to make my life unmanageable and often dangerous, for myself and my children.

Look carefully at your life, is it the life you are proud of. How fun are you to be around? How proud are your children of the way you are living? What kind of role model are you for your daughter who may follow in your footsteps into addiction to men, or to your sons who have to suffer the backlash of your failed dreams and fantasies. What kind of future are you setting for your sons as you assure them daily that males are assholes, jerks, and dicks?

Write below the sentence below, that can start your pathway to serenity and sanity.

I admit my life is out of control.

STEP TWO

ACCEPTED that there is a HIGER POWER that can restore sanity and serenity to my life.

The Twelve Step Prayer is part of a longer poem: However the powerful words of this prayer help millions to overcome their own shortcomings and to learn to rely on the faith and power that faith opens for them in a Higher Power.

GOD, Grant me the courage to change the things I can, the serenity to accept the things I cannot change, and the wisdom to know the difference.

When you are ready to take this step, you are not committing to more than the realization that there is HOPE.

You can stop looking for a man to answer all your prayers and problems. You can stop being angry and disappointed when no man can be GOD. Men are men, not GOD.

STEP THREE

Made a decision to turn my will and my life over to GOD, as I understand GOD to be. MADE A DECISION:

Life is filled with decisions. Every moment you are making decisions, whether aware of it or not.

It is time, in Step Three to look at your life and take control. Make a decision that you are aware of. Make a decision to turn your will and life over to God, as YOU understand GOD to be.

Write some thoughts here. What do you think about God? Where did those beliefs come from? Talk to others, talk to those who seem serene, and fully into their programs, wise and courageous. What do THEY think about a Higher Power, Consider. Make your own choice.

STEP FOUR

A searching and fearless inventory of myself. Look back to the previous pages and figure out who are you, this is NOT an easy thing to do.

First, it takes honesty.

Denial has to be acknowledged and discarded.

Be ready to accept YOUR responsibility for YOUR life one hundred percent.

To make a searching inventor of oneself, it is necessary to find out who gave you the standards you judge yourself and others by.

Fearless means it is important to not allow yourself to be afraid to admit the things you have done that you are ashamed of, that have hurt others, that have hurt you. Look hard at yourself, work with a sponsor, or therapist, or both. Discuss with friends. It takes courage to ask others what they really see in and about you. It takes honesty and courage to look at those comments and make DECISIONS about your own acceptance and responsibility in each situation.

STEP FIVE

ADMITTED to GOD, to my self and to at least one other human being the exact nature of our wrongs.

In addition to men, this Step means looking at all those men that you have harmed. Maybe they harmed you too, but this Step is NOT about balancing the books, it is about clearing your own slate.

This Step is about admitting how much you have harmed your children and yourself. Selecting the wrong man, over and over or refusing to accept the right man because he is not making all your fantasies come true is harming your children, you and the men.

Whether emotional instability or the real physical abuse your children may have suffered in YOUR quest for the knight in shining armor, this step is the scary Step of admitting you have harmed your children.

Use this page to write some of your thoughts.

STEP SIX

I am entirely ready for GOD to remove all these defects of character.

YOU are not going to stop being addicted to dick. GOD can remove your defects of character that have allowed you to give yourself permission to harm yourself, your children and others, but YOU are going to have to be entirely ready to ask GOD to remove those defects.

This step is about getting ready.

Write below and on the next page, in journals, in notebooks, talk to friends, sponsors, family and therapists. THEN move to Step Seven.

Additional writing room for Step Six.

STEP SEVEN

I HUMBLY asked GOD to remove my shortcomings.

This step is important. This step is important. YOU have to realize, God is NOT a vending machine, put in confession and prayer, take our a perfect life.

When you have completed STEP SIX, it might take months, you are ready to say this tiny prayer with honesty and commitment.

Heartfelt.

When you feel yourself slipping, return to Step Six, call your sponsors, pray. If you have to return to Step One. This is a plan for life, not a quick fix for the rest of your life.

You, the same as any other type of addict, have assigned the responsibility to someone, or something who does not exist. Some therapists call this "making magic". IF I just find the "right" man, my life will be perfect. IF you find the wrong man, it will be hell. It is your choice. There is NO man who is going to fulfill you, meet ALL your fantasies, and make you happy. It is up to YOU to BE happy. Abraham Lincoln is alleged to have said we are as happy as we make up our minds to be.

You cannot demand from GOD, you cannot manipulate GOD, you cannot make deals with GOD, YOU have to be ready to HUMBLY ask GOD to remove your defects and shortcomings. There is an old joke about the person who asks GOD for patience, and then demands "and hurry". HUMBLY ask GOD to help and heal you.

Write below the problems, doubts, and questions you have with this step, share them with your sponsor, a therapist, and the group if you attend one.

STEP EIGHT

Make a list of all those I have harmed and think about how I can make amends to them. While this is not about Y O U, make sure to list yourself. Women involved in abusive relationships have first of all harmed themselves.

This step is for those I have harmed. It HURTS your children, especially if you are allowing them to be molested, tortured, abused and or murdered or watch abuse to their siblings. It HURTS your parents, friends, sisters and law enforcement officers, doctors, emergency staff and paramedics to see what is going on. It HURTS news media crews and staff, it HURTS those who see these horrible realities and can do NOTHING to help if YOU will not stand up for yourself and your children.

It is about healing those I have harmed, and healing myself as I realize it is NOT all about me.

Write, write, write.

Some women have needed to buy journalSSSS, but get it all down. Think about every entry, think about the ways I can make amends.

For children it is suggested you find a really good and reliable family healing therapist. I suggest using the Dr. Phil website and ask for suggestions of therapists and groups in your area.

Remember to include those I have harmed by not standing up for myself, or asking for help and allowing someone to treat me in an abusive manner.

Remember that harming yourself in many ways harms others, and make amends to ALL.

Write here, get notebooks, and journals and write until you are ready to make the amends.

Suggestions: DO NOT attempt to say ONE word about how YOU suffered. That is the same old harm to others. Write a letter to the police, paramedics, and emergency rooms and even if not signed, let them know you are thanking them for their help and hope they continue to urge women to get help, for themselves and their children, even if they do not take the advice, it will stay on the mind until acted upon.

Write a letter to a media crew and let them know their concern helped you to realize it was not about "poor little abused me" it was about finding out that people want to help and are HARMED by seeing these situations and now knowing how to help. That their concern did come through and you thank them for giving you strength.

Moms, sisters, best friends: Invite them out to tea, expensive wonderful formal tea, and give them some flowers, and just say sorry. This step means you are owning how much your allowing yourself to be hurt and to let your children be hurt has harmed them. These are the women who love you, and have stood by them, even when you insisted, THEY just did not understand your man.

STEP NINE

I make direct amends to those people where and when that will not further hurt them, or others.

Put your plans from Step Eight into reality. Each successful amend will help you have courage for the hardest one, healing your children and yourself.

Write a list below, Add to it as new thoughts occur. ASK someone else if amends is something that will not further hurt that person. In the end, YOU have to make the decision, but ASK for feedback, and remember NO ONE is forced to forgive you, or like you, or excuse you. YOU are going to NEED to learn to make amends to heal yourself.

Write thoughts, lists, and experiences to remember if you should fall off your path and need to make amends again, or to read BEFORE you fall off your path and remind yourself to not harm others.

STEP TEN

I continue to take constant personal inventory and when I am wrong, I promptly admit it and make my amends.

I learn how to live in the present.

I learn to stop creating fantasies about what life is and how I am interacting with those around me.

For those with Addiction to dick this often means keeping up to the minute on the way we are treating the children, and others in close personal relationship.

The goal is to get up in the morning with a commitment to keep current in life, and to go to sleep peacefully at night knowing we are still peaceful and serene with our own actions.

We can NOT change others, we can only change ourselves.

Write some ways to keep yourself current. Meditation daily

Time for self evaluation to look at your life in current reality and make changes as needed, not wait for chaos or drama to force changes.

Make posters (with your children and others you live with) on how each of you can make home life happier and safer for everyone. Make some rule posters, and review them regularly. Example: TALK about issues, do NOT go to name calling, drama, violence

Find some books for families, and / or groups or classes where several families are working out the same current life programs.

One suggestion is five quiet moments, twice each day. TALK to your children about the need for these, and you will be amazed at the calm and better relationships in your household. IF you wake your children with a kiss, and a time for five quiet moments, whether they sleep, or just lie quietly, it will give their day a better start than the usual screaming, threatening and other bad beginnings to a day children suffer. It will start YOUR day better to take five quiet moments BEFORE it is time to wake up the children. SET out YOUR clothing for the morning. The children see you doing it, and will begin to do this themselves. How much less stressful to get up, wash, and put on clothing than to get screamed out of bed, resist personal health, and then have the stress of deciding what to wear. There are HUNDREDS of family support books, and classes that teach this kind of positive family building.

More thoughts on keeping current:

STEP ELEVEN

I will seek GOD (as to MY understanding of Higher Power) daily, through prayer and meditation. I will seek to improve my conscious contact with GOD as I understand GOD to be. Praying only for knowledge of GOD's will and the power to carry it out.

STOP!!!

Consider this Step carefully.

In America, we have freedom of religion, NOT freedom from religion, whether an atheist or some fanatic, there are 320 MILLION American people who have a right to figure this complex relationship for themselves. Because we have that freedom, we owe the responsibility to respect the religions, or no religions of others completely.

Yet we say we are a country under GOD. Without defining or fencing in what that means to cause divisions among the people of America. Native Americans believe that we dance here for only a short time, in the eyes of our Creator, we are less than a shooting star, but as amazing, unique and wonderful. It is up to each of us to figure out the answer to the question of our relationship to a Higher Power and to respect the rights of others to do the same.

Prayer is not treating God like a vending machine said one Priest I knew. Put in prayer, get out usually selfish material items. Prayer does NOT guarantee the answer we want, one Pastor said, God always answers prayer, sometimes the answer is wait, sometimes the answer is NO, and sometimes the answer is YES.

Prayer is not a magical mantra to force the universe to give us what we demand.

This Step says to LEARN to pray, from the heart, to gain closer knowledge of GOD and the will of GOD as we perceive it, and the courage and serenity to accept and carry out that will.

READ. GO TO MEETINGS. PRAY. TALK TO SPONSORS. TALK TO THOSE WHO YOU SEE AS SERENE AND GROWING IN THIS STEP. TALK TO THOSE WHO HAVE CONQUERED FOR THE MOMENT THEIR OWN SHORTCOMINGS.

STOP!!!!

DO NOT allow others to tell you who GOD is, or what GOD has in mind for YOU. How do you know if you are getting closer?

Like breathing, you will learn, and it will become easier and more automatic. It feels much better to breathe naturally than to try and let someone else tell you how to breathe, and when to breathe. It will feel natural and balanced for YOU when you learn to live naturally with GOD as you understand GOD to be.

NOTE:!! Many criminals, and veterans I have worked with have told me that GOD does NOT want to hear from them for all the bad they have done. I remember one girl at a class I was teaching for a probation department, I asked each youth to say I am WONDERFUL, because God created me, and then tell us something unique and wonderful they liked about themselves. One young woman got so angry and was so incapable of doing this I actually felt as if, as in the Exorcist, her head would spin and she would spew vomit. She finally screamed at me, YOU DO NOT KNOW what I have done. I never did ask. I prayed as I often do, for an anwer:

I said, "did the sun come up this morning", she looked at me like I was demented. The other probations students all stared. She said grudgingly that it had. I said, "is it likely to come up tomorrow", she said yes. I then told her that adult humans every single day allow ten thousand children to starve to death across the world, while America itself, throws away enough food to feed ALL of them. I said, we adults have crime, war, and create situations such as freeways and go out and murder others day after day, yet GOD forgives us and gives us a new day, each day, with the chance to change and create a better world for those we harm. I said WHAT could you possibly have done that is worse than starving babies, killing innocent people in wars and crime and all the rest of the mean things adults to every single day. She said, My name is.........and I am wonderful and found something she was unique and thankful to GOD for giving her. A few days later the probation supervisor called me and said the school had called him and asked what he had done, this girl was night and day. He said not much, just took her to a class where they teach about the sun coming up every day.

GOD loves each of us. I believe from that tiny perfect gift to the whole world, it takes us a very short time to make every human aware that they are too fat, too short, too tall, too skinny, too old, too something and some incredible product will make them perfect, not to mention the manufacturers rich.

GOD is there for you, but YOU have to be there for yourself. And you have to let GOD in. Whatever that means to your, whatever religion or not religion you feel is the most supportive and comforting to you.

Write about these thoughts here.

I believe that without breath, we can not live, and like breath, GOD is totally not concerned with what name we put on, or how we direct it, we can not live without it. I find that many atheists are very good people, who value their relationship to the world, and maybe in their unbelief find a strength they need. It is NOT up to us to decide for them, or anyone to decide for us. VISIT religious communities. Find friends and celebrate with them, or not celebrate with them (Not all religions have the same celebrations). Not everyone has to be a ME clone for me to be happy. That is one of the hardest lessons to learn in life. Our Founders and the Constitution tell us it is IMPORTANT to exercise the RESPONSIBILITY of letting everyone make their own choices.

STEP TWELVE

Having awakened myself, I will share these spiritual awakenings with others who are still suffering. I will do all I can to help others find serenity and the spiritual courage to enjoy and give back to the world GOD has given us.

STOP!!!

This is where you pass it forward. All those who gave you their experience, their pain, their growth, to help YOU heal, give it back to others who can pass it along.

STOP!!!

This is NOT where you, like the reformed smoker we all are annoyed with, set about annoying everyone who dares to come near you, or is unfortunate enough to be stuck on an elevator, plane, train, or in a waiting room with you as you self righteously dump your new ideals on them.

This IS where YOU walk the walk, talk the talk, and by your example of being serene, courageous and wise, draw others towards you.

This IS where you see the suffering of others, whether in your own form of addiction or another and OFFER to do what you can to lead them to the HOPE of finding their own healing. YOU can carry the principles you have learned to others.

Additional page for notes on Step Twelve

SEVEN DAYS TO CHANGE YOUR LIFE

This is based on a program to quit smoking that has circulated around the internet for so many years it has lost its origins. THIS form was written into the original Addicted to Dick book in 2006, but has additions to raise the issues of protecting childreni from being tortured, molested and murdered by their Mother's boyfriend, and a special note for veterans, men, women and transgendered, who have lost their children (and often spouses) due to PTSD related violence and need Court Mandated programs.

The name of the doctor who originally wrote it long ago disappeared into the internet. Our veteran, first responder, and high risk youth and family programs utilized our own therapists, psychiatrists, and human development group specialists to work WITH the women (and now veterans, first responders and high risk youth families) to help the program be a greater self help program for use WITH our groups.

This program is used to help people make lifestyle changes with the power of GOD to break down the walls of their own making, or of the reality that kept them imprisoned in a negative and unsuccessful lifestyle Often people do not even know that they are doing the things that harm their own lives and those of those who love them.

Each of the parts is given its own page, the rest of the page is for YOU to write on, to doodle on, to help get through the first week, to reboot your own inner computer to think more positively and to help you build an inner road map to success.

DAY ONE

SET A DATE with YOURSELF. PLAN to keep that date. It is so disrespectful to not keep dates, or to be late. Treat yourself with respect.

SET that date seven days from day one, WRITE IT ON THE CALENDAR with a time. Read each part of the plan pages, and start today, on day one to do each step of the planAs you read through the seven day plan, you will realize you may already be planning to set that date FARRRRRRRRR, FARRRRRRR in the future. Set that date seven days from today.

THIS IS NOT A New Year's Resolution, if you fail, stop a minute, not an hour, not a day, and start again.

THIS IS NOT A DIET.

THIS IS NOT A HABIT BREAKER PLAN.

This is a date with yourself. You are not even sure yet when, or where, or what you will be moving in to on that date. Do each day's exercises and get to that date with yourself in seven days, ON TIME. Set alarms on your phone, on your computer, on your tablet.

DAY TWO

Pray today. Pray each day for the next six days, start your DATE day with a prayer. You will have built a good habit of praying each day. Just five minutes of quiet, when you wake up and before you go to sleep is enough. It is up to you to decide what you want to do in your prayer time.

Build some prayer time outside, the yard, the park, the mountains, the beach, any place where nature and GOD can be experienced and heard by YOU. It helps to find out how amazing the world is, and remember the ONE who created it all, including ourselves.

DO NOT PRAY for anything you want, desire, or think you SHOULD pray for. Just BE with GOD for a prayer time YOU decide.

Remind yourself, GOD is not a vending machine, put in prayer, get out what you want. Remind yourself that GOD always answers prayer, sometime the answer is yes, other times the answer is wait, and sometimes the answer is NO. Learn to accept it with peace of mind and love.

Since this is a book about relationships with men, do NOT pray for a change in the man, or a new man who is perfect, or any prayer related to a relationship. Prayer for a better relationship with GOD.

PRAY MEDITATE LISTEN to GOD, hear what GOD has to say to you. In the book of JOB, God replies to Job out of the whispering of the wind and the rambling of the creek.
In Haiti, Cuba and other native cultures the greeting one gives to each person is NOT hi, or how are you. The greeting is

"what do you have to teach me today?" Listen to whispers from GOD in those you see and meet along the day.

You may be very out of touch with listening to anyone, or anything but your own fantasies and demans........LISTEN.

DAY THREE

Starting from Day three, for the rest of your life, create and continue the habit of eating something RAW everytime you eat even a bite of something.

This book is about addiction to men, but it may be surprising to find out how many times a day you are munching, and to take a realistic view of WHAT you are eating. A cup of tea without sugar or a cup of coffee without sugar, cream, or any other additive is NOT considered eating. EVERYTHING else is. Get prepared. Create a LARGE container of cleaned, ready to eat raw foods. Vegetables, fruits, and nuts. Set out a jar of nuts and dried fruits and raisins in an easy to reach place. Eat at least one tablespoon every single time you put anything else in your mouth. Eat RAW vegetables BEFORE sitting down to eat a meal.

The positive pledge to eat something raw every time you put something into your mouth, brings into focus how you are treating yourself.

The addition of a few grapes, apple slices, a carrot, or even a small salad help you to realize when and what your are eating, and fill you up before you attack that pizza or bowl of ice cream.

Another suggestion was to chew a piece of gum, BEFORE eating the raw item, and then drink a 16 ounce glass of water, wait five minutes and see if you in fact actually want that snack, cookie, or candy bar. Write down your experience and give it focus for an interesting as well as self growth health investigation.

DAY FOUR

A brisk walk each day.

EVEN if you live in a bad area, or only have time to walk when it is dark and the kids are asleep, design a little walk way for yourself and have a brisk walk around your house. It is of course fine to take a walk on your tread mill, but out in nature, greeting others, looking at your neighborhood, seeing you might help, they are old, lonely, disabled, need a ride to the store, need a hand cleaning once a week or so, or just someone to say HI to as you speed by on your brisk walk.

Spend time with yourself, and with GOD, and finding out how much you resist even this small amount of exercise.

DAY FIVE

Do something nice for yourself. DAILY This is an interesting part of the plan.

Make a list of nice things to do for yourself. Choose on if you have a hard time thinking of one each day. DO NOT MAKE THIS ABOUT MONEY. It does not count to get on the phone and buy yourself something on a credit card. Go in and give yourself a facial, learn to love your own face, just the way it is. It is OK to buy yourself something, but this should NOT be the focus of this part of the plan. IF buying things is part of the chaos of your life, use NOT buying as something nice for yourself, or send a check to pay off a bill you have been avoiding as a something nice once in awhile.

When was the last time you merely took the time to sit and brush your hair, or sit with a face mask on for the full time noted on the packaging. Enjoy the feel of the brush, instead of focusing on how you look, and what you wish looked different.

Think about the blessing of having hair. Enjoy it for a moment instead of hating your hair because it does NOT look like the hairstyles, and wigs, and extensions professionally placed on models for commercials, movies and music videos.

GO TO BED EARLY. Scrunch your toes around in the blankets, find the most comfortable place, meditate and fall asleep.

GET UP A LITTLE EARLY. Instead of leaping out of bed at a screeching alarm on the tenth snooze setting, and screaming at the kids to HURRY, and attempting to find clothing, get showered, dressed, and out the door, just get up a little early.

Meditate for five quiet moments, pray, arrange your clothing, shower, do your hair, and when the alarm goes off, go kiss the kids and ask them to do THEIR five quiet moments and be ready for breakfast in fifteen minutes.

SAY NO. If you do NOT want to go to Grandma's for a holiday, or a cousin you never met wedding, funeral, or kids high school graduation, say NO. YOU do not owe anyone an explanation. Just be dependable and reasonable enough that when you say no, people know you have a good reason. It is none of their business that you just need a go to bed early night, or stay in pajamas Saturday. This does NOT mean if your Dad or Mom is sick you do not be there and supportive in as much of a way as you can.

SAY YES. Make a list, and look for opportunities. Do NOT go to that long distance relatives kids graduation when YOU are asked by a friend to go to a play, or out to dinner, or just to go sit on the beach in the sunset. Say YES to a new class, a new book, or just a tea with a friend for FUN, not because either of you has drama to hash over and over.

DAY SIX

Do something nice for someone else.

As you are addicted to men, something nice might be to NOT discuss your drama with anyone and everyone unlucky enough to find themselves near you, whether it is victimization or being "in love" spare someone.

Possibly you might make a list of ALL those who have listened to you, and go LISTEN to them about anything, even if it is a blow by blow account of the cartoon they just watched.

Do something nice for someone you do NOT expect a payback from.

Something you do not even expect a thank you for. A great example is to NOT raise that triumphant finger at the person who just cut you off and nearly made you crash on the freeway. Just take a deep breath and drive safely.

Something you can do with no one knowing you were the one who did it. A great place is to donate small toys, and blankets to paramedics, firefighters, and police to give to children who they constantly are rescuing that have to spend a scary time in a police station or emergency room waiting for "someone" to come get them.

Think of something YOU wanted from Santa, but did not get. Open that thing, and explore it. Then rewrap it perfectly, and donate it to a community toy drive. Many first responders have Christmas Eve programs where they go out with the emergency vehicles and have Santa to deliver toys and stocking. Fill ten or twenty stocking with candy, art materials, small toys and donate them for first responders who have to work on Christmas Eve, people get in accidents, and their children are scared and afraid as they wait for Social Services to find someone to come and pick them up. How fun to have a stocking from Santa, even if their religion does not practice Christmas......it is the love and hope that you are packing.

There are many NOT doing things that are nice for other people. This is NOT about giving to charity to show how nice you are. It is about learning to give in many ways to BE as nice as you might be.

This might include NOT giving your positive word of criticism on the clothing they are wearing or the food they chose to bring for lunch, or a potluck.

This might include NOT talking about your latest romance, to your new romance, or to anyone who will listen, we are not thirteen forever.

This might include listening and hugging and NOT offering suggestions to a family member or friend. Once a friend and I sat with another friend and her daughter in law on the night her son had been killed on the freeway on the way home from work. We dug our fingernails into each others hands to keep from crying and running out. Years later my friend told me, that of all those coming to see them, we were the only ones who just sat and let them remember how wonderful he had been. It really hurt to hear how much he loved them, and how much they loved him. But it was FOR them, not for us to go pay our duty.

Go drop by a bouquet of flowers and a nice cheese and cracker platter to a disabled neighbor and sit down and LISTEN for a moment. Wave hi to them every day as you jog with your dog. It means more than you will ever know.

DAY SEVEN

This is the hardest part of this plan

To read over your pages, to think over your experiences, and to create your own plan for the rest of your life to keep the positive changes that have come into your life growing and going. They may, or may not have certain direction.

Since this book is about women addicted to men, you are probably going to have to begin to set some ideas in place to help you heal and never get into another man mess.

This is NOT the day to promise to give up men.

This is NOT the day to promise to be "perfect" whatever that means, and be that perfect self forever.

This is the day you make a PROMISE to GOD that you will make a commitment to GOD that you believe that GOD has the power to bring down the walls of your own actions and consequences. That you will LISTEN to GOD to find a plan, the promise and the path for YOU that will lead to what you wanted all the time. Peace, harmony and joy. To love and honor yourself, to be loved and honored in life. If that brings a partner, a person who will honor and love you, that will happen in GOD's time, not your demanded time. It will be in GOD's way, not in response to your fantasies and demands.

If you can not make this promise on Day Seven go back over the seven steps of the plan, continue the five active days of the plan for another few days, set a new DATE with yourself in five days. Review and make your commitment, or review the five days again, and set a new date five days each time. Make your commitment. Do not quit on yourself.

IN CONCLUSION:

These pages have given two plans that may help women who are addicted to men take a look at themselves, and own the reason for their unhappiness and endangering themselves and their children. The reasons for the out of control downward spiral of their lives, for the hurt and emotional emptiness they spew on to their children, along with the emotional, mental and physical harm inflicted on the children by their boyfriends. For the molesting, torture, abuse and death inflicted on these innocent children by their boyfriends.

These women are often victims of domestic violence because they are so blinded by their fantasy of finding the "perfect" man they refuse to look at the reality of the men they choose. The often are found to be SURE that love can fix it all, and that they will be the woman who will change a seriously defective man. The idea that they can "change" a man with enough "love" is too enticing to get many women to admit to the violence, and harm to themselves and their children. The physical abuse is the tip of the iceberg. Emotional, financial, mental and other forms of abuse are added, but women who are addicted to men WILL not face the realities and often become so beaten down by the abuses they no longer can escape the abusive relationship.

It is necessary and sad to mention that many women are inflicted with a religious or family "duty" to stick by her man. The conclusion of the authors of this book, and the major domestic violence programs is that GOD never created anyone to be abused, mentally, physically, emotionally, or financially and surely did not put any child on this earth to suffer unspeakable abuse, torture, and death at the hands of the Mother's fantasy or religious mores.

There are also women who know how to recognize men who may be dangerous to them, to wait to know a man well enough to know his friends, his family and others who are able to let her know who he really is. There are a small number of women who do marry a man who through some crisis, or PTSD, or other situation change and become unexpectedly dangerous. Women need to know the signs, and not feel obligated to put up with abuse, or abuse to their children. A woman is able to give loving good bye to a man, letting him know, this is not about love, it is about I and the children, deserve to BE SAFE.

In the original Addicted to Dick stories of real women were included, not by name or any recognizable part of their story. This book does not contain those stories. We do however ask that women join groups and share their experiences to know that they are not the "only" one, and that other women have survived abuse, and saved their children from abuse, molesting and death from boyfriends, or even fathers of their children.

The profits from the books, and classes are given to allow the programs to be offered free, or at lowest cost possible to ALL women in Court Mandated programs, or who BEFORE they are arrested, and their children taken away want to change their lives for their own safety and happiness and to protect their children.

ARE THERE SUCCESS STORIES:

YES, otherwise we would not have taken the time or expense to re-write this book, and give hope. YES, and in groups, YOU can share YOUR success and help others wherever you, or they are on the path to healing.

OTHER BOOKS BY AUTHOR

Reassessing and Restructuring Public Agencies: What to do to save our Country

Carousel Horse-a teaching inclusive book about equine therapy

Spirit Horse II: Equine therapy manuals and workbooks

Could This Be Magic- a VERY short book about the time I spent with VAN HALEN Dollars in the Streets-Lydia Caceres Edited by Author about first woman horse trainer at Belmont Park

Addicted to Dick –a healing book quasi Twelve Step for women with addiction to mean men

Addicted to Dick-2018 Edition Self help and training manual for women who allow men to torture, molest and kill their children

Books to be released:

America CAN live happily ever after: first in series of Americans resolving all the issues

America CAN live happily ever after 2: Second in series of HOW to go out and BE equal, and to part of the OF the, BY the and FOR the People our Constitution guarantees us. If the school is not teaching your children, go down and read, do math, join a science project, do lunchtime Scouting for the kids, go sit in the hallways with your smart phone and take lovely action video for the parents of kids who do not behave. More. Many suggestions from parents, and how to fundraise.

Carousel Two: Equinc therapy for veterans

Still Spinning: Equine therapy for women veterans

Legal Ethics: An Oxymoron???

Friend Bird: A children's book about loneliness and how to conquer it (adults will love it too)

Kids Anonymous and Kids Jr. quasi twelve step books for and by youth and teens

12 Steps Back from Betrayal from Brothers at Arms and 12 Steps Home two quasi twelve step books and work books created by author and veterans, and author's Father for Native American and other veterans

BIG LIZ: The Leader of the Gang Racial Tension and Gang Abatement work by author

PLEASE join the tee shirt contests by checking the web sites on the books and contacting the link provided. WE love children, teens and adults helping us to give our classes free, and spread the word of our work. ALL of our work is done through education projects by our high risk youth, veterans and first responders page NATIONAL HOMES FOR HEROES/SPIRIT HORSE II. We are just getting back to full work due to cancer of the two Directors and vehicle accidents and our stable burning down in a forest fire a couple of years ago. We promise to get more organized as we move along. 2019is our first year of taking nominations and awarding a Keiry Equine Therapy Award. We will also need poster and tee shirt designs for that. See Carousel Horse and Spirit Horse II links to nominate a program. God bless us, as Tiny Tim said, Everyone.

Printed in the United States
By Bookmasters